REVIEWS

"This book will break your heart...and then fill it to overflowing with the powers of love, hope, resilience, and amazing strength. Diane opens herself and her life to readers with honesty and hope. Your heart will, in turn, respond to Diane's story and her victory."

—Nancy Rasmussen
Memoir Teacher, Coach, Editor

Celebrated author Diane Davis expertly shares an imitate, raw, and honest page-turner allowing us to deeply feel her heartbreaking life challenges and hard-fought wins of happiness! *Tragic Victory: Learning to Navigate Life in Tough Times* is a survivor's powerful, riveting, and inspiring journey through deep loss and major disappointments. A triumphant road map of hope, perseverance, and living your best life beyond adversity.

—Renee S. Clark
US Army Veteran and Retired Federal Civilian

"My eyes swelled with tears after the first few pages and I couldn't put it down. I felt the deep hurt, maternal distress, and I became lost in this mother's story, the tragedy unfolding. This first book from Diane Davis managed to surpass my high expectations AND blew my mind. This is definitely a must read for those who have suffered, are suffering, or need to learn how to grow from the devastating experiences of their lives. We can learn a lot about how to navigate in tough times!"

—Sharon Manker, M.Ed.
Award-Winning Supply Chain, Supplier Diversity & Inclusion
Strategist, Author, and Keynote Speaker

"Diane Davis shares her story of unimaginable loss and the transforming power of love with grace and an open heart. It is my honor to know this extraordinary lady and to have witnessed her rise from utter despair to joy and affirmation, from tragedy to victory, and even more."

—Georgia Garnsey
Author, Freelance Writer

"Diane Davis' reflections on the loss of both of her children is a contemplation on grief transformed into inspiration for everyone with the privilege of learning her story. Her journey is testament to taking life—especially at its darkest moments—one step at a time towards grace, gratitude, and even joy... and then sharing that lived experience to help others do the same. Written with honesty and balance, Tragic Victory is her gift to us all."

—Eileen Ruby
Private Investor

"I met Diane while taking pictures of Taj playing tee-ball shortly after his arrival in Philadelphia. I was immediately drawn to Diane and we have been friends ever since. She is one of the strongest, kindest, and most vibrant women I know and her confidence and optimism are truly heartening. Her tale is one of unimaginable loss, adversity and struggle but the reader does not get consumed by the tragedy. Instead, Diane's words lift the reader out of the despair and onto the journey of strength, courage, and love. Diane's victories are an inspiration to others who might also be struggling or struck by tragedy, and an uplifting message to never give up, to find the strength to carry on, and to keep living.

—Kate Riccardi
Kate Riccardi Photography

DIANE DAVIS

TRAGIC VICTORY

Learning to Navigate Life in Tough Times

A Memoir

Foreword by Monica McGrath, Ph.D.

ELOHAI INTERNATIONAL
PUBLISHING & MEDIA

Published by ELOHAI International Publishing & Media:
P.O. Box 1883
Cypress, TX 77410
elohaipublishing.com

For inquiries or to request bulk copies, email hello@elohaiintl.com.
Photos by Kate Riccardi: katericcardiphotography.com

ISBN: 978-1-953535-54-2

Printed in the United States of America

DEDICATION

I dedicate this book to my two late children, Chemaine Diane Johnson "Chemmie," who couldn't fight the monster of addiction but had a light inside her that shined brighter than the sun. My son Scott Stephen Johnson "Scotty," who struggled with alcoholism, but loved life and made his mark with his short-lived years.

I dedicate this book to the two loves of my life, my beloved husband Ron Davis and our adored and precious grandson Taj Davis. My husband walked this journey with me, held my hand when I didn't know if I could go forward, lifted me up, and encouraged me. He would always say "don't quit" and he promised to love me each day!

My daughter left us the gift of Taj, an incredible, kind, caring, and loving young man who gave us purpose. A true blessing, a gift, and a victory. Our reason for survival.

TABLE OF CONTENTS

ACKNOWLEDGMENTS

As I begin these acknowledgments I'd first like to thank my parents John and Lucille Johnson, God rest their souls. They made me the person I am today and I stand on their shoulders. I lost my mother, my rock, at age fifty-two to breast cancer. But, she and my father provided for me and my sister and they loved their two grandchildren. They gave me courage and strength to be who I am today.

My husband Ron, the love of my life and life partner of twenty-six years is the most committed and loving man one could ever know. A very loving father and grandfather, he has walked this journey with me with unending support. Thank you for your help, guidance, and love with this book, suggesting, lifting me up and forever encouraging me. There were times when I felt I couldn't go on but he gently would say, "You can do this, just keep writing and don't quit."

My most sincere gratitude and special thanks to my extended family for all of their prayers, encouragement, love, and support.

A special thank you to Taj Davis, our amazing and incredible grandson, for his unwavering support.

ELOHAI International—Natasha Brown Watson, author, publisher, minister, and CEO of ELOHAI International Publishing and Media. Several months ago I picked up my phone and gave Natasha a call out of the blue not expecting an answer. But when she picked up I explained I was writing this book. She listened carefully. We spoke with each other many times and finally she asked me to send a chapter of the book. I humbly thank Natasha for all of her patience, guidance, and care with me. She is very responsive and positive. The spirit of her soul is inspiring. She ignites a creative spark in people that attracts them toward her. Thank you Natasha for publishing my book and giving me your weekly prayers and support.

To ELOHAI International Author Program Director Elisa Everts, thanks for your unwavering patience, understanding, and guidance throughout this process.

A profound thank you to my writing group led by Nancy Rasmussen, my writing coach, who formed a group of supportive women. These women guided me through the process of writing my memoir and gave me valuable feedback and have now become dear friends; Kristbjorg Eide, Marian Forman, Paula Jones, Ellen Sinoff, and of course Nancy herself. I am deeply and humbly grateful to these women for all of their love and support while working on this book.

To Monica McGrath, my daily walking companion who was with me when I first received that dreaded phone call, I give my heartfelt thank you. She has been with me throughout the years and has always been encouraging and supportive. She has always been just a phone call away. She is a special and dear friend.

To Michael Bradley, my computer expert who has helped me with formatting and typing. He has traveled miles even enduring inclement weather and the rest of life's hurdles to help me realize this book. He has been with me since the start of creating this memoir. You have helped me depict things in vivid detail and added a flourish of color to my writing. You have given me uplifting thoughts and have been encouraging throughout this process. You are a dear and special friend.

To Cara Orfanelli, another dynamic computer expert, friend, and neighbor, with no hesitation, she is always there whenever I have a question.

Lastly I give thanks to God for allowing me to write this book. *Give thanks to the Lord for he is good. His love endures forever.* Psalm136.1

FOREWORD

I doubt you will ever meet anyone as special as Diane Davis. Let me introduce you. And no, it's not just her obvious courage, endless energy, and unflagging commitment to her family that set her apart from others; it's also the unique spirit she brings to these pages. Her spirit is revealed as you read. You'll see it in her open heart, her steely strength, her ability to stay open to the world, and her willingness to face and conquer what could crush others, her victory.

She writes this book for all of us who are asked to face the realities and uncertainties of life and the sometimes tragic turns we never expect. Diane inspires us to open our hearts to others, to commit ourselves to what matters most, and to give our hearts to life—no matter what life hands us.

Diane was my personal trainer when we met almost twenty years ago. And, as a personal trainer she had the uncanny ability to read my moods, cajole me when I would falter, and push me when she could see I needed to be pushed.

She is a skilled communicator, an expert in her craft as a fitness instructor, and an inspiration to me with her abundance of personal energy. She trained clients in every age group and at every stage of health and took me as I prepared for a high-altitude hike. Everyone she has trained benefits from her ability to coach, motivate, and challenge us to go beyond what we thought was possible for ourselves.

All these skills and characteristics, high-energy, optimism, a strong and powerful voice, and the ability to motivate excellence in others, are the ingredients that form the foundation upon which she builds this book and shares her story and message of hope.

Yes, her story, told on these pages, is painful and frightening for parents everywhere. But her losses are not unique, and her children's struggles are shared by many. The research tells us that approximately forty-six percent of U.S. adults today reported having dealt with substance abuse in their families. Every year the numbers of parents who lose their children to addiction climb ever higher.

Diane's story takes us on a journey through her early days as a new mother, the hardships as a single parent, and eventually her gift of finding a loving relationship and marriage to a strong and supportive partner. The backdrops through all this are the painful realities of her children's struggles.

Throughout this story, I promise you will see personal insight, strength, resilience, and inspiration as well as the love that she emanates.

I believe you too will find Diane to be a unique and special woman.

These pages will both break your heart and heal your heart. In this story, there is a pathway that will help all of us face adversity and learn how to gather support for the isolation of grief, despair, and loneliness.

Diane's story is not at all finished. Today she resonates with her energy, and she is alive with commitment to a beloved grandson and husband, to her work, and to her extended family and friends.

She continues to build a life of meaning with grace, and an open and loving heart.

As you read her story, let her reach out her hand and bring you along with her as she drives toward the future, no matter what burden you carry, I encourage you to walk with her and see how this unique and special woman will help you see beyond what you think is possible.

Monica McGrath, Ph.D.
Leadership Consultant
Educator
www.drmonicamcgrath.com

CHAPTER 1

LOSING MY DAUGHTER

Wednesday, February 10, 2010

I wish I could still hear her voice, the voice of my daughter who would always say, "Hi Mom, it's your daughter!" You don't know pain until you crave a conversation with someone no longer alive.

What happened? That question rings in the mind of any parent whose child is taken over by a substance and leaves before her time. Gone too soon. Parents do their best to give their children wings to fly and roots to grow, but sometimes the roots grow in the wrong direction.

Chemaine Diane Johnson, my daughter, was her name. She gave birth to a son, Taj Kemper.

One morning Taj got up to go to school. As he was looking for his mommy, he saw her sleeping on the couch. "Mommy, wake up! Mommy, wake up!" But his mommy didn't wake up. Mommy had gone to sleep forever.

Little five-year-old Taj picked up the phone off the floor, next to the couch where his mommy lay, and called her boyfriend. "Mommy won't wake up. Mommy won't wake up." Mommy's boyfriend, Bo Braxton, rushed over to her apartment, but mommy was gone. Bo called 911. The police, ambulance, and coroner all arrived before the eyes of frightened little Taj.

Chemaine lived in Honolulu, Hawaii. She left the Bay Area to explore life on the Hawaiian island, Oahu. Life for Chemaine was a series of ups and downs, more downs than ups. Jobs, no job. Not always having a place to live, smoking pot along with cocaine, which became her drug of choice. Chemaine suffered from severe asthma. One evening Bo gave Chemaine a pill to help with her asthma. Then they shared a joint and a few lines of coke. Bo went home. Chemaine fell asleep on the couch. The pill, pot, and coke stopped her heart, and she never woke up.

I was living in Philadelphia with my husband Ron. We had moved from the San Francisco Bay area in order for Ron to take a new job in Philadelphia. I was a personal trainer for Buttonwood Square condos where we lived.

It was a snowy winter morning in Philly that day. A blizzard of a storm, snowing sideways. I was training my neighbor Monica in the condo gym. My phone rang. It was early, 9:00 a.m. in Philly. I saw that the area code was 808. "Oh my goodness, it's six hours earlier in Honolulu!"

"Hello Bo, is everything OK...?"

"No, um, No um."

"What is it Bo? You're scaring me... Is Taj all right? Is Chemaine all right?"

"Um, Chemaine is dead."

"WHAT... WHAT...WHAT ARE YOU SAYING?"

I became hysterical. Monica tried to calm me down and took the phone. She heard the horrible tragic news and gently put her hand on my shoulder; I was in shock and close to passing out.

Chemaine, my beautiful daughter, was dead. I did not know how to process this tragedy, it couldn't be happening. I had already lost a child; I lost my son eight years earlier in an accidental drowning. My mind was racing and confused. There was a blizzard outside, and Ron was upstairs. I had to get to Ron. Monica and I headed to my apartment. I was slow and listless, moving like a zombie. Ron was working from home on this storm-driven day. He was devastated to hear the gut-wrenching news and began a barrage of questions I was not ready for: "What happened? What about Taj? Where is he? Who has him?" Monica took over. With a total blizzard in Philly, I could not get a flight to Honolulu for two days. I had to wait. What about Taj?

I was in a state of chaotic confusion. My mind, body, and spirit were completely scattered, but Monica was very calming and helped settle me down to ask the necessary questions about Taj. Who could take care of him until I arrived in Honolulu? I immediately thought of Chemaine's boyfriend, Bo. Taj would be in good hands with Bo until my flight arrived. After a number of phone calls, I discovered that Bo had a criminal record and would not be allowed to take Taj. SHOCK! What now?

Chemaine belonged to the Salvation Army Drug and Rehabilitation program. She attended meetings to keep herself straight and on track. She had a wonderful chaplain there, Chaplain Jan, who worked tirelessly with Chemaine. Sometimes Chemaine stopped attending meetings, but Jan would always reach out and bring her back. At that moment I thought of Chaplain Jan, and her relationship with my daughter. We had several conversations about Chemaine. I had met Jan and had a deep respect for her. And so, I called Jan with the tragic news that Chemaine was dead. She was devastated and began to cry. I was also crying uncontrollably. Catching my breath, I explained that Bo had a criminal record and could not take care of Taj until I got there.

"There's a blizzard in Philly, and I can't get a flight for two days!"

"Not to worry, I will take care of Taj," replied Chaplain Jan.

I cried harder, but was so relieved that Taj would be safe. Chaplain Jan went to pick up Taj and brought him to her home. She slept on the floor next to Taj in her bed so that he wouldn't be frightened. She kept him safe and calm until I could get to him.

I called Steve, Chemaine's father, my voice weak and shaky. It was three hours earlier in Sausalito, California, where he lived.

"What's up?" Steve asked sleepily as he heard my voice, all but a whisper.

"I have some very sad news for you," my voice quivered. "Chemaine is dead." There was silence on the other end.

"What happened?" He immediately added, "What about Taj?"

"Bo cannot take care of Taj, he has a record," I exclaimed. "Chaplain Jan will take care of him until we can get there. There is a blizzard here in Philly, and I cannot get a flight out for two days."

I described the circumstances around our daughter's death and got off the phone, no longer able to keep my composure.

The blizzard finally calmed in Philly. Monica made flight arrangements for me to fly to Honolulu via San Francisco. I met Steve at the San Francisco airport, and we flew to Honolulu. It was a long five-hour flight across the ocean. Many thoughts of Chemaine, her childhood and why this might have happened flooded my head. Steve and I had been divorced twenty years, but maintained a very good relationship. We had both remarried. I struggled with where did I go wrong, what did I do, and how I could have helped prevent this horrible tragedy.

Finally, we arrived in Honolulu and went straight to the Hilton Hawaiian Village Hotel. It was early afternoon. I called Jan immediately from the hotel.

"I'm here," I said in a nervous breath, "how's Taj?"

"He's fine! I've been with him every minute, and we'll be over in an hour," she replied.

I thanked Jan profusely, and explained that Chemaine's father Steve had come with me. We waited in the lobby of the hotel for Taj's arrival. I couldn't sit still, and paced the entire hour.

CHAPTER 2

LEAVING HONOLULU AND FINDING BROTHERLY LOVE

S uddenly, I saw Chaplain Jan and Taj. Taj looked so scared and lost as he slowly walked up the ramp holding Jan's hand. His pants legs were rolled up so he wouldn't trip, and he looked like a little waif! Taj saw me as I began running to meet him. I picked him up and hugged him so tight and kept saying how much I loved him.

Taj and I were very close; I had even cut his umbilical cord when he was born. I had never missed one day talking to him by phone in Honolulu. Taj had a special name for me, his grandmother, Mimi. Steve was called Grandpa. Grandpa gave Taj big hugs too! He adored Taj and had brought him a dinosaur. Taj loved dinosaurs. We assured Taj everything was going to be alright.

The next day Steve and I went to Social Services with proof showing we were Taj's biological grandparents. A difficult process to leave Honolulu with Taj began. We just wanted to get Taj settled as soon as possible, but we had to wait until all of the papers cleared. I was anxious to get back to Philly. Also, before we could leave, we had one more challenge. We had to face Chemaine's apartment and gather her belongings.

I called Chemaine's landlord to explain what had happened. The landlord was very sympathetic. He liked Chemaine and thought she was beautiful, sweet, and kind. He'd often hear her sing and admired her voice. He asked us to come by the next morning to pick up the key to her apartment.

Entering Chemaine's apartment was completely devastating. How could someone live like this? How did Taj survive this? What had happened to my daughter? It was dirty and soiled, there was trash everywhere. My daughter had totally spiraled down, down to death. I think she wanted to be a memory.

Steve and I began cleaning up, picking up photos to save, toys and books that were meaningful to Taj. Eventually, I became overwhelmed with the clean-up and decided the apartment management could complete the cleaning. It was just too much.

I wanted to see Chemaine to say my final goodbye. Steve did not want to see her. I acquiesced, and we decided to have her cremated. Chaplain Jan arranged for us to have a service at the Salvation Army Chapel before leaving. She gave an eloquent eulogy to my daughter. The service was small and beautiful with several friends of Chemaine's that loved her. Despite my anger with him, I understood when Bo came to the service to say his goodbyes. Saying goodbye did not lift the devastating and profound loss I felt.

I was in touch with Ron several times a day. He was preparing for Taj and me to return. While there was a room for Taj in Philly, Ron bought a blow-up mattress to put next to our bed so that Taj wouldn't feel alone and frightened.

Finally, after three days of waiting, a victory! I became Taj's guardian, and we were free to leave Honolulu!

Ron was lovingly known as Grandbear by Taj. Grandbear is truly a GRANDBEAR...a big, strong, gentle, kind, former NFL football player with a heart larger than life itself. He was waiting for us at the airport gate with open arms. Taj ran to him! Grandbear carried Taj and didn't put him down until we arrived at the car. Taj was wide eyed and curious, but felt safe in the arms of his Grandbear. He seemed lost, but we kept telling him over and over how much we loved him. He had just lost his mother and didn't truly understand that this was his new home.

Taj slept in our bedroom for six months on the blow-up mattress. We felt he needed the continued knowledge that we were right there for him. He had periodic nightmares and was often jarred awake by the unfamiliar and loud noises of the city. Admittedly, it also made me feel safe knowing as long as he was beside us nothing bad would happen. However, that didn't stop us from lying awake at night with our minds racing: What about school? What about sports? How would he make new friends? He was extremely shy and quiet.

Monica and her daughter, Kaitlyn, worked tirelessly while I was in Honolulu preparing a "how to" booklet for Taj. Schools, parks and rec, where to go, how to get there, who to call. I was so relieved and completely touched by the beauty of this gift. Everything was color coded, labeled, and tagged. There were no words that could ever say "thank you" enough.

Ron and I found the perfect preschool for Taj. The Caring Center! A victory! The preschool represented its name. We told his story to the principal and the teachers, who all listened intensely. Some teared up, and Taj was showered with love and affection. We knew it was the right place to provide the safe and understanding environment he needed.

Then we immediately went to Fairmount Sports and signed Taj up for T-Ball. Taj loved to play ball; Grandbear began tossing the ball to Taj before he could crawl. His first coach, Michelle, took him under her wing, saw his natural talent, and cultivated that into his lifelong love of baseball.

And so life began for Taj in Philly and a new life for Ron and me!

But how had this all come to be? How had the past brought us to this final goodbye, and into the future of raising Taj?

CHAPTER 3

CHEMAINE'S YOUTH

Monday, March 4, 1968, 10:07 a.m.

She was flawless at birth! She had perfect features, with creamy skin, hair so long it covered her face. I had always wanted to be a mother. A blessing! Becoming a parent was a victory.

As Chemaine grew up she became complex and difficult. At times very moody, even at a young age, she seemed to have different personalities. She was also a daddy's girl. Daddy was everything! Whatever Chemaine wanted, Daddy would give her.

Steve and I separated when Chemaine was five years old, and her brother Scott was two. Separation and divorce, along with my mother dying of breast cancer, made it a very difficult time. The kids didn't understand, especially Chemaine. Why wasn't Daddy coming home?

We were living on the army base at the Presidio of San Francisco, when I learned my mother had stage four breast cancer. Steve was a captain in the Army. He had recently returned from a tour in Vietnam. He wasn't the same, and things did not work between us anymore. I decided I had to help take care of my mother, so I took the kids and moved back home with my parents in Denver, Colorado.

Going to stay with my parents was extremely difficult because they didn't believe in separation or divorce. You "stay together" no matter the circumstances, for the sake of the children. Living at home was unbearable, and there was constant tension in the household. Mom was suffering with her illness, vomiting several times a day, physically exhausted and very weak. Cancer was taking over her body and still she was determinedly begging me not to get a divorce from Steve.

My father also made living in the house hard. He was an alcoholic with a hair-trigger temper. He would freak out if Scott touched or broke anything. At times Chemaine would have horrific temper tantrums. My nerves were on edge. I told my father that I needed to get help, and see a psychiatrist. His reply was that only "crazy people" see psychiatrists. I decided I had to leave my parents' home, but where could I go with my two kids?

Gigi and Woody Garnsey were good friends I had met during my marriage. Steve and Woody had gone to school together. The Garnseys' invited me and the kids to move into their basement. I took them up on their offer and made the move. It gave me peace of mind and closeness with my kids. The Garnseys' were very loving and understanding. They helped find the right schools for Chemaine and Scott.

We lived in the Garnseys' basement for six months. The basement wasn't finished, but it was comfortable and warm. Gigi helped me find a job at the Children's Museum of Denver. Finally, I could provide a place for me and the children. We could be in our own apartment. A victory! The apartment was bright and airy with lots of windows. I could hear the birds chirp in the morning. I loved that sound, and the kids were happy to have their own space. I was forever grateful for Gigi and Woody.

Elementary school was exhilarating for Chemaine. She liked her teachers. She loved to wear pretty dresses, go to birthday parties with her friends, and have fun. However, sometimes it was difficult being black in a predominantly white school. Chemaine had a café latte complexion with long black curly hair. Some teachers would refer to her as the "little black girl." Chemaine was too young to understand the implication. I tried to explain to her about the differences in people and skin tones. I went to the school and asked the teachers about their comments. They danced around their statements. It was distressing being a black, single parent in the suburbs of Denver, Colorado.

During this time my mother succumbed to breast cancer. She was only fifty-two years old. My father became helpless and lost. Like most women, my mother did everything; she was the matriarch of the family. She was beautiful, honest, and caring, a loving mother and grandmother. I was devastated. For my entire life she had been my best friend and confidante. My father and I had a wonderful, uplifting funeral for my mother at New Hope Baptist Church in Denver. In attendance were all of the congregation, along with her siblings, five sisters and four brothers. My mother had been the youngest, the baby. We laid her to rest at Fairmount Cemetery and Mausoleum, a beautiful place to visit, meditate, and recall memories. I always place flowers on the crypt when I visit to let her know that she is loved and remembered. I had lost my support, my rock. Now what?

For months I had struggled with the idea of returning to Marin County, California. Steve lived there, and he could assist me with the care of the children. Maybe life would be easier for me, Chemaine, and Scotty. So, with much trepidation we packed up and left Denver. We set up our lives in Tiburon, a beautiful town across the Golden Gate Bridge from San Francisco, where I enrolled the children in school.

Chemaine, a middle-schooler, became a cheerleader and joined the school choir. She loved to sing and often landed a lead singing role in school plays. She would practice with the cheerleaders and band for hours. Singing and dancing made her happy. She also began noticing boys.

In high school, she continued cheerleading and singing. However, her friends became very influential. We argued about her choice of friends, and she began to rebel. I noticed personality changes with

Chemaine. She started to experiment with pot, cut school, and ignored her curfew. Our arguments became more frequent and intense. At one point I worried that Chemaine wouldn't graduate from high school.

Chemaine wanted her father to be more present in her life. I knew a lot of her acting out was to try and get his attention. Steve was there for Chemaine, but he had remarried. Compounding matters, Chemaine and his new wife did not get along. Chemaine was very possessive of her father. She wouldn't have gotten along with any woman in his life.

Chemaine graduated from high school and decided to delay going to college. Her dream was to attend Juilliard, the private performing arts school in New York. She wanted to sing and dance more than anything. She wanted her name "up in lights on Broadway!" Chemaine went through extensive preparations for tryouts at Juilliard, and we flew to New York for auditions. This was a huge opportunity for Chemaine. She was understandably nervous. She'd practiced for days. I was a wreck. Could she handle this momentous change in life? Could she someday be on Broadway?

It seemed like hours as I waited while Chemaine was behind big closed doors waiting her turn to audition. Finally she came out. I jumped up! "How are you?" "What was it like?" "How did you do?" Chemaine was exhausted and said she didn't know. She thought it went all right, but there were lots of talented people and good auditions. We went back to the hotel and waited anxiously to hear. She would find out the next day if she could move on to the finals.

The next day we toured New York. It was a nice change to just be fun and upbeat! As we returned to our hotel room the phone rang. I answered and the voice on the other end asked for Chemaine. I gave her the phone, my hand shaking as I held my breath. Chemaine listened carefully and said little. "Yes, I understand, thank you," she said and hung up the phone. She looked at me with watery eyes and said,

"I didn't make the cut. I won't move on to the finals." My heart sank. Juilliard told Chemaine she could continue with her voice training for ten thousand dollars. I didn't have that kind of money. Chemaine said, "Daddy will pay." She immediately called her father. Steve said, "No." Chemaine was devastated. Little did I know this would change Chemaine forever. A tragedy.

CHAPTER 4

RAMEN NOODLES—LIVING IN MARIN COUNTY, CALIFORNIA

When we moved to Tiburon, Chemaine was ten, and Scotty was seven. Raising my children became all consuming. I tirelessly worked different jobs, starting out as a receptionist for Independent Blue Cross in San Francisco. I arranged all airline travel for the top executives of the company and hand-wrote their airline tickets. (That was back in the day!) The pay wasn't great, but I could pay rent and buy groceries. From Blue Cross, I landed a job with a start-up travel agency in Larkspur, California, closer to home. The pay was better but with longer hours. After I was on the job for six months, the company went bankrupt. What now? I was out of work and worried about surviving with two kids. I had to file for unemployment and food stamps. Food stamps were so embarrassing in my mind. How would I shop with them? When would I go to the grocery store so the neighbors couldn't see me? I had to find another job.

Two very good girlfriends, Judy Barr and Jane Boussina, helped me search for jobs to apply for. An opportunity came for me to interview with the radio station KJAZ to do voice-over and radio sales. It was located in Alameda, California, across the San Rafael Bridge and an hour and a half commute each way. I loved speaking and had an excellent voice. It was perfect! I wanted this job. I had gone through interviews one and two, with the third and final interview with the President of KJAZ. I got the job! A victory!

I enjoyed the daily drive from Tiburon to Alameda. Being on the air was exhilarating. I loved every minute and felt on top of the world. One morning as I parked my car, the director of KJAZ was arriving at the same time. He approached me getting out of my car and asked if I'd meet him for a drink that evening. I was stunned and unsure why he'd ask me for a drink. He was married with two kids. I stammered and stumbled with my words and said, "No thank you." He persisted asking me out for weeks until I became uneasy, nervous, and a little scared. It was disturbing. After several weeks, I decided to speak with the president. Surely, he would protect me from this seeming predator.

I had an early morning appointment to see Mr. Wilkerson. I was nervous, and the palms of my hands were sweaty. His office was large and perfectly decorated with awards and plaques from all over the United States covering the walls. I waited for half an hour before being called in and had developed a terrible stomach ache. My mouth was dry as I began to try and explain that his director, Sunny Buxton, was asking me for drinks. I told him that it made me very uncomfortable. He listened and seemed to be understanding and compassionate. I didn't feel great about the meeting, but I thought I was safe.

The next morning, after I arrived at the station, I was called into Mr. Wilkerson's office. He very politely asked me to pack up my desk, that I was no longer needed. What a gut punch. What do you mean? Tears began to well in my eyes. What did I do wrong? I just got this job, I loved it, and I was doing great. How would I pay the rent and feed my kids? I was devastated and sick to my stomach. I thought he'd protect me, but it was the "good ole boys club." I didn't play the game with Mr. Buxton, and I had to pay the price. I was fired.

Wow, back to the unemployment office and back on food stamps. I had no savings. It was embarrassing. The food stamp allowance was minimal. I had enough for milk, bread, cereal, eggs, hamburger, and

Top Ramen noodles. The noodles were filling for the kids, and they liked the different flavors. It was a nightly menu. I grew to hate them.

I filled out applications and went on endless interviews. It was difficult trying to interview for jobs with Chemaine and Scott, especially during the summer. Babysitting was expensive, and I had no relatives close by. Steve was helpful but he worked and couldn't take time off for me to job search. He had the kids every other weekend and would take them for a week to ten days in the summer which was helpful. However, the months went by slowly. I was frustrated, and money was low. My kids were depending on me, and it was up to me to provide for them.

I slipped into a state of depression. Why was this happening to me? I couldn't climb out of the pity pot. Wasn't I deserving of a life with dignity? Was it because I was black? Was it because I lived in Marin County? There were very few black people in Marin County. It was tough being black in a white world. Had I been white, would it have been different for me and for my children? What was good for some wasn't good for me.

I was a woman who always displayed the comportment necessary for the situation. My diction was perfect. I didn't speak Ebonics, black slang. My parents were demanding about my sister and me speaking properly. Growing up we were often complimented on how we spoke. We had to enunciate our words perfectly. In the work world, clients would often mistake me for being white on the phone, but when they met me there was sometimes a hidden look of surprise (though they tried not to show it). I was used to it. It didn't bother me, but it didn't make me feel good either. I was attractive, proud of myself and my accomplishments. So, I stopped licking my wounds, got up, held my head high, put on my blazer, zipped my pencil skirt, picked up my briefcase, and marched in for my next interview.

Finally, after eight months, I was offered a job with Gray Line Tours of San Francisco as director of sales. A victory. Three months later, I was promoted to vice president of sales and given a staff. I was happy. No more food stamps and no more Top Ramen. After being with Gray Line Tours for five years, I got an offer to work with the San Francisco Convention and Visitors Bureau. My hard work was paying off. My career was booming, and I was feeling good about myself. The kids were getting older. Chemaine was searching for herself. Scotty was a senior in high school and applying to the University of California, Berkeley.

CHAPTER 5

CHEMAINE'S YOUNGER BROTHER SCOTT

Monday, July 19, 1971, 11:23 a.m.

Scott (Scotty as we called him) was born at 7 pounds and 14 ounces, a little feisty bundle with fists tightly clinched. He was a beautiful baby boy, Chemaine's brother. They were three years apart in age and very close. As Scotty grew up he looked up to his sister. He loved school and began to play soccer at three years old. He was very determined, bright, smart and made friends easily.

Throughout elementary and middle school he found a home on the soccer field. He was given the nickname Scooter, because he was very fast, low to the ground, and ran like lightning. In high school he won seventeen soccer matches. He loved being a goalie! Scotty was also on the debate team in both middle and high school. He loved to present arguments and was very convincing.

He developed a love for languages, especially French. Scotty carried on his study of French in high school but also studied Spanish and Russian and spoke all three languages fluently. His mind was brilliant. He held a part time job in high school and bought himself a red scooter. It matched his nickname, and he loved it.

Scotty always kept an eye out for his sister, and they often had long talks. I wished I could have been a fly on the wall and heard their conversations. He didn't think some of his sister's boyfriends were good enough for her. Chemaine listened, but she was very strong willed and followed her own instincts.

Our Christmases were special with just the three of us. We decorated the tree, had hot chocolate, played Christmas music, and danced. It was festive, warm, and wonderful to be together. Scotty gave me beautiful gifts—dresses, scarves, and jewelry. There's an old saying that boys love their mommas. Scotty loved me and his sister.

As a senior in high school he decided that he wanted to attend college in California. He fell in love with the University of California, Berkeley, his first and only choice. He loved the campus, the surroundings, the kids and the little town of Berkeley itself. It had a bohemian feel. There was no convincing him to explore other California universities. He filled out applications, wrote essays, and submitted them all. There was a long wait until he received word. He would attend UC Berkeley! He was the happiest I'd ever seen him. It was a dream come true, a victory. Scotty was truly our prize. No one in our extended family had graduated from college. A few cousins had gotten in the door, but had not made it to the end.

His years at UC Berkeley were good years. He played soccer, loved his classes, and continued studying languages. He took lots of math classes, trigonometry, geometry, physics, and chemistry. He also loved to sing and took up playing the guitar. By his second year, he had decided to move to his own apartment. Chemaine and Scotty had both moved away; I was an empty nester. The house felt strange but I got used to it. Scotty would visit often to check on me. He would give me rides on his red scooter, which always made me nervous.

On May 26, 1994, Scotty graduated from the University of California, Berkeley. Where had the time gone? It was such an achievement for him to graduate from such a prestigious school. Graduation day was grand. The campus, with all its pomp and circumstance, was aglow. We were all there, Steve, Chemaine, Ron, and me. All so proud! His name was called to receive his diploma, and as he walked across the stage, I wept; I couldn't believe my eyes, my son. What a victory.

Soon after graduation, Scotty became an options trader for O'Connor & Company, in San Francisco. The hours were early, long, and intense, but he thrived on the yelling and screaming of numbers, the chaos on the stock exchange floor. The stock market was all consuming with lots of pressure.

After a few years as an options trader, Scotty was offered a partnership with the firm Gill Trading at the Pacific Coast Stock Exchange. The pressure increased, and he began to drink. I was worried because he wasn't himself, and his personality had changed. He was exhausted, and didn't call me much. When I called him, he was short with me and quickly ended the conversation. What was happening? Scotty had always been the child I could rely on, our golden child. I feared without help he would become like his sister. A tragedy.

CHAPTER 6

CHEMAINE'S DOWNFALL

After the Juilliard heartbreak, Chemaine seemed to spiral downward, jumping from one boyfriend to another. She began to lose weight and didn't seem like herself. I would come home from work and find weird people in the house. It was all very upsetting.

I tried to talk to Steve and explain that I thought Chemaine was addicted to drugs. Chemaine's behavior had become so erratic I was actually afraid of her at times. One evening I found a knife under the couch pillow. Oh God, was she going to hurt me? She would disappear for days. I would be frantic, never knowing where she was, if she were alive or dead. I told Chemaine that if she didn't change her lifestyle, she couldn't continue to live at home.

Finally, I had to ask Chemaine for the keys to our house. I told her not to come back. "What do you mean?" Chemaine asked. I decided I had to show tough love. What is tough love? It's a decision that rips a parent's guts right out. I couldn't live with her, and I couldn't live without her. A tragedy. I didn't hear from Chemaine for over a year. For me, every day meant not knowing where she was, how she was living, and I was always afraid that answering the phone could be devastating or worse, "that call."

I talked with Steve; he was supportive but angry with Chemaine's behavior. He paid for several rehabs, and it was really up to Chemaine if she chose to survive. I was overwhelmed with worry and fear. I had two beautiful children struggling to make their mark in the world. How could I help them make it better? I read article after article about drug addiction and spoke with professionals. At times I was frantic. When I would receive a phone call from Chemaine or Scott I would always say how much I loved them.

I kept a strong voice and presence for my children. Sometimes, no matter what I tried, it seemed as if the walls were closing in on me. Fear would set in and take over my entire being. I felt alone in the world with no one on my side. I needed someone to lean on and support me. Someone, somebody who would reassure me that I was doing my best, that I was doing enough. I didn't want this to end in a tragedy.

CHAPTER 7

MEETING RON

I had been divorced for twenty years, had a great job with the San Francisco Convention and Visitors Bureau (SFCVB), owned my home in Corte Madera, California, and drove a black BMW convertible with "Sweet DJ" on the license plate. I was a successful single mother with no intentions of getting married again. My job allowed me to travel across the United States. During these travels I would work to entice other cities to bring their conventions to San Francisco. During a trip to Atlanta with the Director of Sales from the San Francisco Hilton we met with the Vice President of Sales at the Atlanta Hilton. The result of the meeting was a victory. Atlanta agreed to bring its convention to San Francisco.

After the last meeting I simply wanted to return to my hotel, have room service, and relax, but this particular evening my travel colleague told me that we were going to a nightclub. "Nightclub? I don't think so," was my reply. But, before I knew it, we were in a cab on our way to Mr. V's, a nightclub in Atlanta owned by a famous basketball player, Dominic Wilkins. As we entered the club the strobe lights were flashing wildly. The music was thumping and pumping. My heart started to skip a beat. I wanted to leave immediately. My colleague said he'd take care of me; however, he saw a young lady that caught his eye and he took off. There I was, stranded. What was I to do? I found another friend and told her that I was leaving. As I attempted to make my way to the door a seven foot dude asked me to dance. "No thank you," I said, but he insisted. The guy had a shiny gold-chained medallion hanging around his neck which seemed to blink to every beat of the music. Along with the distraction of the chain, he was missing every other tooth and he'd had a little too much to drink. He looked like a tall monster.

My friend noticed that I was trembling with fear. She asked a gentleman standing next to her to help me. He tapped me on my shoulder and asked me to dance. Again, I declined. He looked up at the seven foot brute and told him that we were together and he had all his teeth! We went to the dance floor, but I had two left feet. I was shaken by the overbearing man. That's how I met Ron. He was my knight at Mr. V's, that night. He was kind, gentle, and helped me to calm down. We all took a cab back to the hotel. Ron and I talked for several hours. The drawback was Ron lived in Washington D.C., and I lived in San Francisco. He was so nice and attractive, but it was geographically undesirable to think of a possible relationship. As the meeting ended we exchanged business cards and flew back to our respective cities.

Ron wrote me beautiful letters and poems. The first present he sent was a music box with a Stevie Wonder tune, "I Just Called To Say I Love You." That was the most beautiful gift I'd ever received. Why was Ron so far away? Why did he live on the other side of the country? I decided not to respond to his calls, because the distance between us was too far and too much.

Our next meeting, by chance, was at the French Embassy in Washington D.C. Neither of us knew the other would be there. Ron's boss had made a last-minute decision for him to attend. The French Embassy was breathtaking as I mingled among the crowd. Suddenly I saw Ron! We seemed to notice each other at the same time. Our eyes were glued on each other, and it seemed no one else was in the room. We inched our way toward each other and gave a gentle hug. I couldn't believe that we had reconnected. We sat together during the symphony. It was magical.

Then it was time for us to depart again and return to our cities. We decided to date long distance. It was difficult. We had late night phone calls that lasted for hours, and we managed to see each other every three to four months. I learned a lot about Ron being a former NFL football player and being drafted out of college by the San Francisco 49ers. It was fascinating! Ron was interviewing across the U.S. to become president or CEO of a convention bureau. He was a finalist in Tampa, Florida. My heart sank. Would he ask me to move to Florida? Could I leave Marin County and my children? I don't think so. Finally he heard the Oakland Convention and Visitor Bureau was searching for a president. He applied and was flown to Oakland for several interviews. Ron landed the job as President and CEO of the Oakland Convention and Visitors Bureau. A victory! Oakland was just across the San Rafael Bridge from Corte Madera, where I lived.

I introduced Ron to Chemaine and Scott. They loved him. It was an instant attraction, as if we'd all known each other forever. We all jelled. Ron had a son, Ron II, attending Virginia State University, Ron's alma mater. He was a computer science major and very smart. He'd already received an offer to work as a scientist on the Naval Base in Virginia Beach. He enjoyed spending time with us. Scott was attending the University of California, Berkeley. Chemaine was figuring out her life and spending time with a boyfriend that didn't have her best interests at heart.

Now Ron and I were dating across the Oakland Bay Bridge rather than across the country. So, we decided to move in together. I was reluctant in the beginning, but Ron said if I didn't mind tripping over big shoes, it could work. Life was good, but we both wanted more. Did we want to spend a lifetime together? He was my soul mate. We couldn't live without each other.

One evening Ron came in from work with a little Tiffany turquoise bag and gave it to me. (Oh, what was in it?) As I began to open the bag I saw a little box. Ron was watching me as I nervously fumbled trying to open it. As I lifted the top I began screaming—it was my engagement ring. It was sparkling and incredibly beautiful. The NFL had not been kind to Ron's knees, but he gently got down on one knee and asked me to marry him. Of course, I said yes! I was over the moon with joy and excitement to spend the rest of my life with this man. After five years we were going to be married. Little did I know that Ron had asked Chemaine and Scott individually if they would give their blessings for us to be married. They were both ecstatic!

CHAPTER 8

THE WEDDING

Friday, July 5, 1996, 6:00 p.m.
Viansa Winery, Sonoma, California

I loved planning our wedding. We both enjoyed driving to Sonoma and Napa Valley, breathing in the winding roads with all their beauty. We had decided Viansa Winery would be the perfect setting for our wedding. We experienced wine tasting and celebrated Ron's last birthday there. Viansa was about a thirty-five minute drive from San Francisco, and it would be an easy drive for guests. The winery sat back high on a hill with amazing views overlooking the vineyards and the valley. It had an Italian atmosphere, almost like being in Tuscany.

Wedding details were easy for me. I found the perfect dress, a fitted bodice over laced pearls. Exquisite! I had one attendant, my dear friend Deena, who would stand with me. My son Scotty would give me away. Ron's father would stand with him. Chemaine was in turmoil with her boyfriend and not sure she'd attend our wedding. My fingers were crossed that she would come, but I had to move on with my life. I selected the menu, table settings, colors, flowers, and cake.

Ron's parents, Emma and Arthur Davis, had never flown on an airplane. We flew them to San Francisco and arranged for them to have a suite at the Fairmont Hotel on Nob Hill. They were overwhelmed with the beauty of the city and the hotel. It was almost too much. Times like this made me nostalgic. I found myself wishing that my parents were alive to take part in the wedding celebration and all of its festivities.

The limousine arrived at precisely 4:00 p.m. It was a sunny, cool, crisp California afternoon with not a cloud in the sky. Ron's parents had not been in a limo before. The voyage was breathtaking for them, so spacious with seats surrounded by windows. There were soft drinks and snacks. My soon-to-be in-laws couldn't believe it. There were *oohs* and *aahs* all along the way. As the driver slowly drove up the winding road to Viansa, they were speechless. The limo stopped in front of two, oversized iron gated doors, the entrance to the Wine Cellar, where Ron and I would be married.

The Wine Cellar was slightly rustic with wine barrels stacked in rows along the wall. My decorator placed gardenias on top of the barrels. The smell of the gardenias over the wine barrels was sensational. Our wedding was small, only sixty five of our closest friends and family. White chairs were perfectly lined up. There was a hearth with a stained glass window where Father William Cullen would stand to unite us. My matron of honor, Deena, arrived along with my son Scott. We all went to change for the ceremony.

At 5:30 p.m., the harpist began to play Felix Mendelssohn's *Wedding March in C Major*. It was such a sweet sound as we waited for the large iron-gated doors to open. At 6:00 p.m. sharp two ushers slowly opened the doors as everyone stood, and my son escorted me down the rose petal aisle to the altar. Ron and I had eyes glued to each other. Father Cullen asked, "Who giveth this woman?" My son said, "I do!" Ron and I both had tears in our eyes. We exchanged our vows repeating scripture after Father Cullen, and we were pronounced husband and wife. He then introduced Mr. and Mrs. Ron Davis to the audience. We'd waited for so long, and the time was just right.

After many hugs and congratulations there was a wine reception in the Market Place at Viansa followed by dinner and dancing under the pavilion. It was all magical! Our first dance was to Stevie Wonder's "Ribbon in the Sky." The guests enjoyed an amazing evening. Memories were etched in our hearts forever. The next morning we flew to Cabo San Lucas for eight days of bliss. A victory. All too soon it was back to reality.

CHAPTER 9

OPPORTUNITY IN PHILADELPHIA

Returning to a normal lifestyle wasn't easy after the exhilaration of the wedding and honeymoon. But things began to settle down. The next few years were busy with Ron and the Oakland CVB, and I returned to work at the San Francisco CVB.

One evening Ron came home and asked me to sit down; we needed to talk. I never liked requests like that; they made me nervous. Had something happened to his mom or dad? No, but he'd received a call from a search firm in Philadelphia. They had received his name in a nationwide search for Senior Vice President of the Philadelphia Convention Center. They wanted to fly him to Philadelphia for an interview. Ron asked what I thought. After a long pause, I said Philadelphia was known for its cheesesteaks, hoagies, and pretzels. I had only been to Philly once to give a presentation about San Francisco. I wasn't sure I'd want to live there. He replied he may not get an offer or he could always turn it down. He was up against over one hundred applicants, so I said, "Why not?" Nothing would probably come of it. And, he'd have an opportunity to see his parents who were aging and lived outside of Philly.

Ron flew to Philadelphia, and the interview went great. He got to see his parents. It made him feel good to see they were doing well. He returned home and a week later he received a call asking him to fly out for another interview. It made me a little anxious. Ron always had great interviews. He was so smart, intelligent, and well read. He called himself a "professional finalist" when it came to job interviews. However, I'd decided I didn't want to move to Philadelphia. We had late night discussions about Philly and the interviews. I could sense Ron wanted to see what might happen and so once again I said, "Why not?."

"See what they say this time, and tell them that you want the kitchen sink," I advised. Ron flew to Philly for a third interview and returned. One week later he received a phone call stating that he was one of five finalists for the position at the Philadelphia Convention Center. Now what? The "what if's" took over. What if they wanted him, what if they made him an offer he couldn't refuse? I had not taken moving to Philadelphia seriously until then. I'd been in California for twenty-five years. Did I want to leave my children, my job? Did I want to leave my friends? I loved living in Marin County. However, it was quite an accomplishment to be one of the top five finalists from the sheer number of applicants. But it would be a huge move, and I wasn't ready.

Two weeks later Ron flew back to Philadelphia. He gave the headhunter ridiculous demands. He wanted a car, a place to live rent free for a year, a half dozen round trip tickets to fly back and forth to San Francisco to settle our home and business. All sorts of crazy stuff! There was a "yes" to everything he asked. Finally Ron said he needed time to talk with his wife and think things over. They told him to take his time, but they needed an answer within ten days. We spent hours and sleepless nights writing the pros and cons about moving to Philadelphia. Ron's parents were aging, and his brothers and sisters lived in the suburbs of Philly as well. Finally, we decided to take the leap. Ron told them we'd make the move. Oh my goodness, what had we done? We would keep our home in Marin County, and we could always move back. Ron had a one-way ticket to Philadelphia on Monday, September 17, 2001. I was staying behind to ready the house for the movers.

On Tuesday, September 11, 2001, Ron was making breakfast downstairs. I was upstairs when I heard frantic breaking news. An airplane had crashed into one of the twin towers in New York City. I screamed for Ron. This couldn't be happening. Ron ran upstairs, and we watched in sheer horror. Oh my God, what was happening? Then another airplane hit the next tower. People were jumping out of windows. I was panic-stricken and sick to my stomach. And, I couldn't reach my kids. Surely the job would be postponed or just go away.

When things began to settle, Ron contacted the Philadelphia office. They told him to proceed as planned. Things were so chaotic, and our nerves were on edge. What we didn't take into account was Ron's ticket was a one way, and with the horrifying events of the past week in the rearview, we did not foresee the inevitable problems this would cause. Ron was detained at the San Francisco airport for hours and missed his flight. He was a tall African-American man and he was drilled over and over again with the same questions. Why did he have a one-way ticket to Philadelphia? What was the purpose for the trip? During the questioning they had taken all of his belongings, his luggage, his wallet, briefcase, and his phone. It was a living nightmare. He wasn't allowed to call me and I was hysterical not hearing from him. Finally, after several calls to Philadelphia he was free to leave. The authorities returned his belongings to him and wished him a good trip. Ron arrived in Philly in the wee hours of the next morning, completely exhausted from the ordeal.

His new job began. All of Ron's requests were granted. They arranged for us to stay in a beautiful long-term, furnished apartment at Buttonwood Square with a fabulous view of Philadelphia. They gave us a car until our car arrived in Philly and provided us with several round-trip tickets to fly back and forth to San Francisco until our home and business were settled.

It was such a new beginning, and we were busy trying to adjust. All along Chemaine and Scotty were heavy on my mind. I established Sundays as our days to call and talk with each other. Sometimes I couldn't reach Chemaine. When I was able to reach Scotty his conversations were short, brief, and sometimes curt. I was worried (in the back of my mind), and wondered if I should have made this move? If I should have left my children? But they were developing their own lives; I had to let go and let God.

CHAPTER 10

BELOVED SON SCOTT

One Sunday morning our phone rang early, it was Scotty. It was three hours earlier in the Bay area. I answered quickly. His voice was low and almost inaudible. His former roommate, Herman, had committed suicide. My voice choked as I swallowed. "I'm so sorry. Are you okay? Do you know what happened?" Scotty said he wasn't okay and began to cry. I knew he was shaken to his core. I slumped over and told him I'd be on the next flight to San Francisco as soon as I could book a seat. I was able to get a flight out that same evening. I had to see Scotty. I had to help him through this tragedy.

He picked me up at the airport, and we went to my hotel to talk. Scotty told me all the gory, grim details of the suicide. I worried how badly this would affect him. We talked for hours and when I looked out the window it was daybreak. We were both exhausted. I stayed for a week, seeing Scotty every day, talking about how he was coping with the loss of his best friend. I talked with Steve and suggested Scotty speak with the Chaplain at Church of Our Saviour. But he didn't want to see anyone. He said he needed time to sort things out. I noticed he was drinking a lot and not sleeping. Fear poured over me. I saw Chemaine and asked her to please check on her brother. She assured me she would.

Finally I had to get back to Philly. I didn't want to leave him. He had a job, which put him under a lot of pressure, and he had his dog, Rudy, who was the most loving dog. I prayed he'd be all right. It was a long flight back to Philly, but so good to see Ron. I was teaching exercise classes at Buttonwood Square, and they helped clear my mind. Ron was enjoying his job. Overall life was good. But we spent many late nights talking about the situation with Scotty and praying he would ask for help.

I was missing Chemaine and Scotty terribly, so in December, 2002, we decided to spend Christmas in San Francisco. San Francisco was beautiful at Christmas, lights gleaming, twinkling, and sparkling. It was like a winter wonderland without snow. We spent three days at the Fairmont Hotel on Nob Hill. It was sheer bliss to hear the cable car bells clinging, and taking in the breathtaking beauty over the entire city. Scotty met us at the hotel the first night for dinner. He was happy to see us, and I was giddy to see him. I noticed his eyes were red, and his pupils seemed dilated. I thought I was imagining things. Chemaine didn't join us for dinner, but we saw her a couple of days later. Finally we moved to a friend's house on Fisherman's Wharf. My girlfriend and her husband were spending Christmas in France and offered us their home. We loved the Wharf with its great seafood, restaurants, sourdough bread, and legendary Ghirardelli chocolate. We felt relaxed and happy.

Christmas morning we went to Steve's home in Sausalito for brunch. It was festive. Chemaine joined us and brought her boyfriend, Rick. Steve didn't like Rick and asked him to leave. It caused tension between Chemaine and her dad. Chemaine was very upset, but we managed to make it through the day.

Scotty had decided to go to rehab for his drinking, and to attend meetings through Alcoholics Anonymous. We were thrilled he'd decided to stop drinking. Scotty decided to stay overnight at his dad's house Christmas night because he had an appointment with the rehab counselor the next morning. After a long and emotional day, Ron and I decided to call it an evening and went back to Fisherman's Wharf.

I called Steve the next morning a little before 8:00 a.m. He told me Scotty had left early to take a drive and go to breakfast. An instant chill came over me. I was rapid fire with questions, "What time did he leave? Where was he going for breakfast? What did he say?" He had an appointment with the rehab counselor at noon in San Rafael. I hung up and called back in less than an hour. Scotty had not returned. I had a pit in the bottom of my stomach. Ron and I got dressed immediately and drove to Steve's home. By then it was 10:30 a.m. with no word from Scotty. No call, no text, nothing. I was anxiously pacing and scared. The hours went by, noon, 1:00 p.m., 2:00 p.m., 4:00 p.m. Something was very wrong. By 5:00 we called the Sausalito police. Hysteria was rising in me, something had happened. The police had received no notifications of missing persons. The hours seemed to creep by. Steve had an antique clock that chimed on the hour. It made me crazy. Ron and I decided to drive back to our place on Fisherman's Wharf. We were silent in the car as we drove across the Golden Gate Bridge. Fear had taken us over. Neither of us could sleep. We prayed the heavenly skies would let Scotty be alive.

Our phone rang at 5:30 a.m. the next morning. We both jumped, knowing that getting a call at that early hour wasn't good news. Scotty's car had been found at Stinson Beach, California, a black 1999 Audi with the keys in the ignition. My heart was pounding so hard that it almost jumped out of my chest. The police told us they thought the person that owned the car had drowned. "Oh my God, what do you mean?" They said there had been a witness and asked us to come to the station. We quickly got dressed. I called Steve, and we met at the Sausalito Police Station.

The witness was kind enough to meet us at the station. She was shaken that she had seen a swimmer taken under by what she thought was an undertow. She gave her recollection of what she'd seen early the previous morning. It had been a storm-driven, windy, torrential rainy day. The waves were heavy and fighting the wind. She saw the swimmer go down and after a few seconds come back up. He too seemed to be fighting the waves. Again the body went down and came back up. Until the last time he went down, he did not come back up. She stood on the side waiting and waiting to see him again, but nothing.

I slumped to the floor. Ron picked me up. The Sausalito police put out a search and rescue for three days. Our good friends Conneen and Dale came from Oakland to help us search for Scotty. We all walked and drove for miles and miles hoping to find any clues that could bring him back. Then the police said it was time to search and recover. His body was never found. Scotty was gone, just like that... my beautiful Scotty, my son, gone. How would I ever get through this? I didn't get to say goodbye.

We belonged to Church of Our Saviour, a small, charming, quaint religious oasis that sits on a hill in the middle of a popular liberal little town, Mill Valley, California. We went to see Father Cullen. He prayed for us and Scotty's soul. We had to try and come to terms with this horrific, tragic loss. I was filled with guilt that we had moved to Philadelphia. I asked Father Cullen if I'd ever smile again and he said, "Most certainly so." We had to gather Scotty's remaining belongings and plan a memorial service.

CHAPTER II

CELEBRATION OF LIFE FOR SCOTT STEPHEN JOHNSON

Friday, January 3, 2003

Wͤe had flown to San Francisco for the Christmas holidays, not to plan a memorial service without a body. I felt as though everything was moving in slow motion, unaware of my surroundings. The church family, immediate family, and close friends helped us reach out to Scotty's friends. Scotty was so loved.

It was a cool, crisp, beautiful clear morning with not a cloud in the sky. Church of Our Saviour has a lovely courtyard with a garden situated outside the church. It holds small benches to sit, meditate, and reflect, surrounded by beautiful flowers. It was a serene, calm and peaceful place to have Scotty's Celebration of Life.

It was an early afternoon service. I greeted guests as they began to arrive. I was consoling others which helped me attempt to stay centered and calm and to focus on others, not myself. Steve gave Scotty's eulogy. It was touching with lots of quiet tears and a touch of humor.

Church of Our Saviour has a crematorium wall. There are several plaques with names of loved ones with their dates of Sunrise and Sunset and inscribed words of loving memory. We placed a special piece of Scotty's clothing in the drawer. The plaque on the outside read, "Our Beloved Son, Scott Stephen Johnson," July 19, 1971 to December 27, 2002. "Son To Stephen Lee Johnson, Son to Diane Johnson

Davis, Stepson to Ronald W. Davis, Sister to Chemaine D. Johnson, Brother to Matthew R. Johnson, Stepson to Virginia Gardner. We Will Love You All The Days Of Our Lives. Rest In Peace."

We had a white dove released that flew up, up, and away high into the sky. I watched until I could see it no more. The poem "I'm Free," was perfect for Scotty.

> Don't grieve for me, for now I'm free
> I'm following the path God laid for me
> I took his hand when I heard Him call
> I turned my back and left it all.
> I could not stay another day
> To laugh, to love, to work or play
> Tasks left undone must stay that way
> I found that place at the close of day.
> If my parting has left a void
> Then fill it with remembered joy.
> A friendship shared, a laugh, a kiss.
> Ah yes, these things, I too will miss.
> Be not burdened with times of sorrow
> I wish you sunshine of tomorrow.
> My life's been full, I've savored much,
> Good friends, good times, a loved one's touch.
> Perhaps my time seemed all too brief,
> Don't lengthen it now with undue grief.
> Lift up your heart and share with me
> God wanted me now, and set me free.

> Author—Unknown

Scotty was more than just a memory. He would live inside me forever. Ron delivered our expression of gratitude and invited guests to a small reception. It was very quiet with lots of hugs, tears, and condolences. We said our thank yous and goodbyes. It was time to return to Philadelphia.

The flight back to Philly was long, somber, and quiet. Ron and I knew what each other was thinking. There were no words to be exchanged.

"Grief is the price we pay for love."

—Queen Elizabeth

CHAPTER 12

FINDING OUR PSYCHOLOGIST

s the red-eye United flight landed in Philadelphia on a
lightly snow-covered morning, Ron and I were completely
drained. The drive to our condo was quiet. I had decided to
go into total hibernation for six months. I was at a standstill and felt
asphyxiated. There was a deep hole in my heart.

Living in mourning is something personal. I thought I would
never get through my heartbreak, but I had to confront it. I was sat-
urated with everyone else's sadness and I wanted to comfort others,
but I didn't know how to help myself. I had to go into hiding and go
to a place where I could mourn without interference. Our home was
my sanctuary with no one allowed to come in. Ron was consoling
and gave me all the space I needed to live with my grief. I felt the
outpouring of love from family and friends during the process of
trying to heal. It was appreciated, but I was wrapped up in my sorrow.

The days and weeks slowly went by. Finally Ron told me that
I had to find someone to talk to. We had to find a psychologist. He
was grieving too. I agreed. I had locked myself away for months, only
going to the gym at 5 a.m. or Whole Foods. When I'd go outside
I was incognito. I didn't want to be recognized by anyone in our
condominium building. I didn't want pity.

It was time to break my silence. I called our primary care phy-
sician, Dr. Gary Dorshimer, and told him what had happened. He
was gentle, kind, and understanding. The next morning he called
and gave me the name of four therapists. He didn't know two of the

therapists well, and he thought two would be very good. The last two were husband and wife. Dr. Dorshimer suggested that I call and try to speak with all of them to get a feeling for their personality and tone. Each time I'd make a call I could hardly explain my pain without sobbing uncontrollably. The first therapist, Dr. Chad Chester, finally returned my call. He was nice but seemed distant. The second therapist, Dr. Shelby Lynn, seemed kind and I thought, maybe. The husband-wife team were phenomenal. They were "It." Dr. Vincent Gioe and his wife Adrienne were both psychologists. I spoke with Ms./Dr. Gioe first. She listened carefully, but didn't say much. Then she gently told me she was deeply sorry for my loss. However, she suggested that I speak with her husband. She felt he was better suited to work with Ron and me. Dr. Gioe called me the next day, and I knew he was the one. We had found our psychologist.

We've been with him for almost twenty years. Care and trust are two major words in my life. Dr. Gioe takes care and trust to another level. He goes beyond the depth of understanding. He's gentle, soft spoken, a compassionate listener, kind, and helps us work through our feelings.

His office is located in an old historic building on Pine Street across from Pennsylvania Hospital, the first public hospital in America. As patients enter his office the furnishings are very comfortable and inviting. He has an oversized brown leather couch in the sitting room, a pleasant and peaceful place for waiting as soft classical music plays in the background. He also has a painting of the San Francisco Golden Gate Bridge on a foggy day hanging on the wall, most nostalgic for me. As we wait to go into the office I stare at that painting which brings back vivid memories.

When he comes around the corner to greet us, we exchange small chit-chat. Then he offers us coffee or tea to have during the course of our session. Ron always asks Dr. Gioe, "Where's the croissants"? Jokingly Dr. Gioe responds, "I'll bring them next time." The office is bright and airy with cushy chairs, healthy green plants, and a large window. I always gaze out the window before sitting, viewing the hospital with its perfectly manicured grounds and beautiful colored flowers. It's breathtaking. We've seen many seasons change over the years from that window. It gives me calm to catch a glimpse of that beauty before starting our conversations.

There were times I felt completely out of control. But, we always left feeling better and calmer after our visits. As the years passed we cut our visits from three times a week down to a weekly visit. Ultimately, we took a break from therapy.

Life was moving along, and I was doing my best to return to society. Dr. Gioe helped me to come out of my shell. It was also helpful to continue my personal training sessions and workout. Being a personal trainer is like being a psychologist. Your clients trust you and share their personal and intimate thoughts. I could focus on someone else other than myself.

Slowly I began to feel better, realizing life would go on with or without me. Visiting with Dr. Gioe gave me and Ron strength. My dear friend Marty Marks, who lives in Tucson, would send me letters and cards weekly with words of inspiration for me to hang on to. She still sends me cards after all these years. Her husband John was also very supportive. My Philly girlfriends, Valerie Furgerson and Delilah Winder, would come to our home, bring food, and sit for hours and visit. Kelly Watson, Iris Fluellen, Amy Sabel, Tom Flynn, my matron of honor Deena Brennan, Conneen and Dale Hooks, and Lovester and Joan Law, were my San Francisco angels who called weekly with words of encouragement, and to say they were thinking of me. With the support of my friends and the sessions with Dr. Gioe I began to see that I could face this head on.

It seemed as if I was beginning to come out of a dark hole. Nine years had passed and I was learning to live with the unimaginable pain of losing my son. And then, unexpected tragedy. I received an early morning phone call that Chemaine had passed away. My special and trusted friend Monica was with me when that dreaded call came. I do not know how I would have made it without her companionship. She played a crucial role in stopping a downward spiral by taking my hand and walking me through the daily steps of life with encouraging words I needed to hear, "You will survive this," and "You will get through this." She was then and still remains my rock to this very day.

Thank goodness for Dr. Gioe. Ron called him, and told him how worried he was for me. I was comatose. Dr. Gioe helped me realize that I had to be strong for Taj, because he needed me. He needed Ron and me. We resumed our visits to Dr. Gioe. During these visits it became clear that I could not retreat from the world like I had before, instead it was vital to be strong.

During all these trials and tribulations Dr. Gioe has been with us, listening and guiding. He is no longer simply our therapist, he's a paragon of balance holding us steady during trying times. He is the gentle force that steers me to breathe when I am reminded of past tragedies. Dr. Gioe was also a stable presence in my life as I weathered Chemaine's ups and downs.

CHAPTER 13

CHEMAINE ATTEMPTS RECOVERY

Chemaine came to me because she finally recognized that she needed help. Steve had paid for four rehabilitation centers, each one more expensive than the last one. Chemaine entered each rehab with the promise that this time would be the "right time." This time she'd remain clean and sober. But, relapse followed relapse. Finally, a "graduation" from rehab number four; she had six months clean and sober. Hallelujah! Such good news! We were all there, front and center: Steve, her brother Scott, Ron, and me of course. It was a beautiful graduation that ended with the prayer of Serenity. Chemaine had it memorized:

> God grant me the serenity to accept the things I cannot change, the courage to change the things I can, and the wisdom to know the difference; living one day at a time, enjoying one moment at a time; accepting hardship as a pathway to peace; taking as Jesus did, the sinful world as it is; trusting that you will make all things right if I surrender to your will, so that I may be reasonably happy in this life and supremely happy with you forever in the next. Amen.
>
> By Reinhold Niebuhr

Chemaine received two blue coins representing six months of sobriety. A victory! The coins were a physical reminder to take life "one day at a time" and to be true to herself during the process of being sober. The coins were meant to celebrate the milestones but to never give up on the journey, the journey to succeed. Chemaine was so proud. She held the coins tight and clasped them to her chest. I cried tears of joy and prayed she'd stay clean and sober this time.

Chemaine got an awesome job with the San Francisco Marriott Hotel in marketing! Her supervisor loved her, and she was on top of the world. Dressing up every day to go to work, she was so happy! Then her friends, from before rehab, slowly started to creep back into her life. Chemaine's personality started to change. She was coming to work late, missing work, and not calling her supervisors to let them know. She was given a verbal warning, a written warning, then placed on probation, and finally released.

She was slipping again, made so much worse by the tragic loss of her brother. Scotty was three years younger than Chemaine, and they were very close, almost speaking their own language as siblings often do. He had tried to warn her off of her bad boyfriends unsuccessfully. She loved and admired him. How could he be gone? Chemaine was in constant turmoil over the loss of her brother and their visceral connection.

One day Chemaine and her boyfriend Bo announced they'd decided to move to Hawaii. Why? I was frantic. Where will you live? What about jobs? My mind was swirling with questions. "We'll figure it out," she answered. They loved living on the island of Oahu. It was beautiful and expensive. However, they bounced from one odd job to another and didn't always have a place to live.

Chemaine landed a job in an architect's office. She was always good with math, and she loved to draw. I was so relieved and proud of her. She started going to the Salvation Army Drug and Rehabilitation program and met Chaplain Jan. She attended meetings every day. I prayed that maybe the meetings would give her the strength to follow through.

Regrettably, she began slipping again—missing work, late to work, or just not showing up. One afternoon I was at the hairdresser when Chemaine called. She was the happiest I'd heard her in a long time. "Hi Mom, it's your daughter, I have some exciting news for you." I held my breath. "I'm pregnant," she exclaimed! She was so happy. I was stunned with mixed emotions about the pregnancy. I never thought Chemaine wanted children, but I had always wanted to be a grandmother. In spite of her addiction issues, I was happy for her and begged her to please take care of herself. Now she had the promise of a new life that she would want to protect and cherish. I didn't want the baby to be born with any health issues. I knew this baby could make a difference, but the demon of addiction was always tapping on Chemaine's shoulder.

Chemaine seemed to have a healthy pregnancy. Ron and I flew to Hawaii several times to see her. She was radiant. However, she was drinking and smoking during her pregnancy. I pleaded with her to stop for the sake of the baby. Then, it was time to make the drive to Queens Hospital, Oahu. It was time for this child to enter the world. Chemaine asked if I would be with her in the delivery room. "Of course I will!" She and Bo were not getting along, and she didn't want him to be part of the delivery. I scrubbed up and followed the doctor into the delivery room. I was a nervous wreck. Chemaine began to push and scream. I urged her to breathe as I held her hand and told her everything would be all right. She pushed again, this time with a louder scream. Taj had entered the world, Thursday, September 30, 2004 at 11:27 p.m. The nurse asked if I'd like to cut his umbilical cord. I said yes. The nurse handed me the scissors. My hands were trembling, but I did it! The nurse wrapped him up in a blanket and handed him to me. I cried as I saw this beautiful new life and then laid him in his mother's arms. We both began crying with joy. Taj was a gift and a victory.

Chemaine said she'd be the best mother. She was in awe of Taj, his tiny fingers and toes and his beautiful mouth forming coo's that one could barely hear. The hospital kept her for three days. She was doing well and anxious to leave. Ron had returned to Philly for work. I was staying an extra week with Chemaine and baby Taj, but I needed to leave soon.

Why was the hospital keeping Chemaine? All indications were that everything was a-okay. One evening as I was sitting in her room holding Taj, a nurse came in and informed us that Taj could not go home with Chemaine. Panic raged over me. I was horrified and said, "What do you mean, why, what's happening?" Drugs had been found in Chemaine's system upon giving birth, and Taj had to be tested for drugs in his system immediately. The nurse took him from my arms quickly and said he'd be placed in a foster care system. My heart was pounding, my stomach was turning over, and Chemaine was crying hysterically. Taj had just been born, and they were taking him away. He was three days old.

I dropped to my knees on the side of Chemaine's bed and began to pray. I asked God to please let Taj be taken care of and that we wouldn't stop until we got him back. I told Chemaine she had to be strong and work hard to prove she was a great mother and they would return Taj to her. That night we packed up her belongings and returned to her apartment. We called the Salvation Army and asked for Chaplain Jan. Luckily she was on duty that evening. We told her what had happened; she too was upset, but she promised to work closely with Chemaine and follow each step to assure Taj's return. I called Ron and he was in shock.

During the week I remained in Honolulu, I made endless trips to Social Services. They wouldn't give me the name of the foster parent but assured me that when the time was right, Taj could be returned to his biological mother.

I had to leave Chemaine. I had to get back to Philadelphia. It was a long and somber flight back. Ron met me at the airport as I nearly collapsed from exhaustion. The days and months ahead were grueling. I spoke with Chemaine daily. Chaplain Jan telephoned Ron and me and said she felt Chemaine should move into the Salvation Army living quarters so that Social Services could see she was working at her rehabilitation program and was serious about being a mother. After six months it was determined that Taj would be returned to his mother. Chemaine had to be supervised at all times, but it was a showering of blessings.

She was allowed to return to work in the architect's office. Chemaine loved her job and she was good at it. Drawing and designing was her gift. She even started singing again. Bo was begging her to move back in with him. Finally, with trepidation, the Salvation Army allowed Taj and her to move back to her apartment with Bo. It wasn't easy getting the baby ready to be taken to daycare in the mornings, going to work, picking him up, making dinner, doing laundry—it all seemed overwhelming. But, she was determined to be the best mother to Taj.

One evening we were talking by phone, and Chemaine asked if Ron and I would take Taj for a while; I was stunned. What do you mean a while? This is your baby that you love so much. She said she felt inundated with responsibility. Needless to say, I thought she was using again. I asked if she was working on her program. Her answer, "Yes Mom." She said her job was good.

Then I asked her straight up, "Are you using again?" With an edge to her voice and an emphatic "No" of defiance, she said she wasn't using. I had that familiar pit in the bottom of my stomach that Chemaine wasn't telling the truth.

As the months passed, I wasn't talking to Chemaine as much. I missed my daily talks with Taj, which were always the highlights of my day. There was a six-hour time difference. When I was able to reach her she sounded strange and distant. I could hear Taj crying in the background. She said she'd been working late, but she was actually going out and leaving Taj with different neighbors, some she didn't even know. I was frantic. I reached out to Chaplain Jan, and she confirmed my worst nightmare—Chemaine was using again. What was I to do?

After many phone calls I finally reached Chemaine and told her we had to talk. I was worried sick about them. Chemaine was quiet and told me she wanted to write me a letter. "A letter, why? Why can't we talk?" She hung up the phone, and I didn't hear from her for over two weeks. I called Chaplain Jan, and she said that Chemaine had completely shut down. She wasn't responding to anyone. Ron and I had sleepless nights and decided we needed to fly back to Honolulu. Just as we were at our wits end, one morning I went to get the mail and there was a letter from Chemaine:

> Dear Mom, I love you very much and I love Ron. If anything should happen to me, I'm asking you and Ron to please take Taj. I know he'll be safe with you. Love, Chemaine

I started sobbing and picked up the phone and called Chemaine. This time she answered. We talked for over an hour. She said she felt it was too much for her to take care of and raise Taj. She wanted to know that he would be in our loving care if something was to happen to her. I assured her that nothing was going to happen to her. I also told her that Ron and I were going to fly back to Honolulu to spend time with them. Chemaine asked me not to come at that time, she needed some space, and to come in a couple of months. She and Bo had started living separately, but they saw each other in the evenings. One evening after Bo left, Chemaine fell asleep, never to wake up.

CHAPTER 14

RISING SON: ADOPTING TAJ

Friday, August 17, 2012 2:23 p.m.
Philadelphia Court of Common Pleas
Family Division

Time passed, Ron and I had waited for over a year for this date to adopt Taj, and to give him our last name, Davis. He had finished first grade, and we wanted to be a complete family.

Our lawyer, Ed McCain, had guided us through the court proceedings. We'd been to court several times; were questioned about Chemaine, her childhood, her lifestyle, and her boyfriends. Ron and I had been through a complete background check. We were questioned intensely about our life, Ron's ex-wife, my ex-husband, our jobs, and our schooling. At times it was exhausting.

It was a cloudy and rainy Friday morning. I was nervous. Ron was always strong and steady. He said everything would be fine. Our lawyer was dynamic and had prepared a good case for the adoption. Judge Monroe entered the courtroom and in a loud voice we heard, "All rise and raise your right hand." My hands were shaking uncontrollably. "You may be seated." The judge asked our attorney to present our final case. This was our fifth time in his courtroom.

Ed was masterful. He spoke of our exemplary character in the community. He told the judge how Ron was a former NFL player, from a great family; how Ron and his brother had gone all through elementary school, high school, and college together. He added that they both were drafted out of college to the NFL, Ron, to the San Francisco 49er's and his brother Art, to the Pittsburgh Steelers. He explained to the judge how Ron was named Father of the Year in 2014, by the Southern Jersey Chamber of Commerce. He explained how Ron had been President and Vice President of several organizations. Ed told the judge about my background and upbringing. How I was from a very spiritual family, a former preschool and elementary school teacher, and a personal trainer for over twenty years. He explained he had received letters from the community regarding our character and how we were great neighbors. Finally, he told the judge that above all we were loving and kind people, that we would be outstanding parents to Taj and give him a good life.

The judge thanked Ed. Then he asked for Ron and me to stand. My knees were knocking. We were asked a series of questions about our feelings for Taj and if we were ready to become parents again. We answered, "Yes!" Judge Monroe then took his gavel, hit the bench, and said, "Request granted. You're now awarded full custody of Taj Scott Johnson Davis." Ron and I were ecstatic about the news. I was crying tears of joy! A victory. We could hardly wait to tell Taj the good news about his name. He was too young to completely understand. But he seemed proud to print his last name Davis on his school papers.

CHAPTER 15

TAJ IN ELEMENTARY SCHOOL

The years ahead were full of joy and excitement for the Davis family. Taj experienced seeing his first snow. Living in Hawaii, he had never seen snow. He had wide eyes and wanted to touch and play with this white stuff. Ron and I bought him a snowsuit and a sled. We went sledding on Lemon Hill. The sound of his laughter filled our hearts. He rolled over and over in the snow, made snowballs, and loved throwing them at us.

Taj attended kindergarten through sixth grade at Russell Byers Charter School. RBCS was a great little school founded by Laurada Byers in loving memory of her husband, Russell. The school was walking distance from where we lived, and they welcomed him with open arms. Taj was very shy and unsure of himself in the beginning. He was helpful with his teachers, but he never wanted to be at the front of the line or in the front row of the classroom. His teachers admired him and thought he was very handsome, sweet, and kind. He made friends easily. Kids were drawn to him.

Taj practiced karate for three years at Marshall Posture Studio of Philadelphia, earning himself a Brown belt. He also learned to play the violin in third and fourth grades, although he preferred to be on a baseball field or basketball court. It was his love of sports that truly expressed his personality. The more he played baseball and basketball, the more he began to open up and become less shy with others.

At Fairmount Sports Association, he played T-Ball, then baseball and basketball. He was named Most Valuable Player (MVP) during several seasons of baseball between 2012 and 2017. (Taj has a special talent in baseball; he pitches left-handed and bats right-handed, a unique ability.)

During fourth grade, Ron and I received a special invitation for the three of us to take a private tour of the West Wing of the White House. Wow, how exciting! The invitation came from a neighbor I had trained for several years. Her daughter worked for President Barack Obama and National Security Advisor Susan Rice.

We decided to take Taj by Amtrak to Washington D.C. Taj had never been on a train. As the train rolled down the tracks, he had such wide eyes, watching all the sights and listening to the sounds. He asked one question after another.

Upon arriving in D.C. we went straight to the Big Red Bus to take a tour of the city. We sat outside on the top deck of the bus so we could see and experience everything. We saw the Lincoln Memorial, Vietnam Memorial, the White House from a distance, the Martin Luther King Memorial, the Washington Monument and much more. It was exciting to see all the sights, but it was a long day. We were worn out and ready to go to our hotel, the Hay-Adams, for dinner and a good night's sleep. It was important to be well rested for the next morning, the big day. Our host, Laura Abrams, would meet us after breakfast and take us to 1600 Pennsylvania Avenue, to tour the West Wing. Once there, we had to go through a checkpoint to be cleared and were given special badges to enter those historic doors. Finally our host was given the "all clear".

It was magical entering the West Wing. It seemed small compared to what you see on television. Seeing the Seal of the United States of America and the pictures of all the past presidents hanging along the walls was more than we could believe. Then there was the Roosevelt Room which had no windows, located in the center of the West Wing, where meetings were held daily.

Then we went up the stairs to the Oval Office, the working office for the President of the United States of America. The room had three large windows, the president's desk, and a fireplace, and was grand. The president's desk was perfectly placed and very neat. The furniture was modest. There were photos of the president's family and the Martin Luther King bus on the back table. It was majestic! This would become a memory etched in our minds forever.

Taj had a great time running up and down the hallways, making our host nervous. I got the hiccups uncontrollably in the Oval Office. My nerves got the best of me. The guard outside the Oval office brought me a glass of water, and I thanked him.

We then went downstairs to the Press Room/Briefing Room where the president and press secretary held their daily briefings. It was awesome standing at the podium where the press secretary stood. We had a great photo op. Then we were taken to the Situation Room where all major decisions are made. The room was breathtaking!

We couldn't believe our tour; it was filled with glee and excitement! Finally we were given three presidential boxes of M&Ms which Barack Obama had signed! Then we were off to lunch and the train back to Philly. Ron and I enjoyed every moment, and Taj had lots to tell his friends about his visit to Washington D.C. When he returned to school the following Monday, his teachers were amazed at how much he had to say and share with the class.

The years seemed to go by quickly. Sixth grade had a tradition for students to scale the outside of the four-story school building if they chose to do so. Taj said he would definitely be one of those students. Ron and I were shocked that Taj was going to scale the wall. The morning arrived, and it was chilly. Several kids lined up to be given instructions for scaling the wall. Safety straps were placed around their shoulders and waists. Then they were led to the roof of the building. The kids seemed so high up as we stood on the playground below, holding our breath.

Taj was up! It seemed to be taking forever as the instructor spoke to him. He stood on the edge of the wall and leaned back. I thought I might faint. Ron was giving him words of encouragement. "You got this, stay focused, you're doing great!" His legs and feet appeared to fling wide and slightly out of control. Finally, his feet touched the ground; I could breathe again. There was thunderous applause, and Taj was smiling from ear to ear. I was crying. Ron ran and hugged Taj. What an accomplishment! Taj was so happy and proud of himself. This was the icing on the cake for sixth grade. A victory.

Taj did well throughout his years at Russell Byers. One of our neighbors, Cara, who we had become very close with, would spend time helping Taj with homework. He made good grades and was often recognized as outstanding student of the quarter. However, as sixth grade came to an end, Ron and I felt it was time for Taj to change schools. Many of his friends had left Russell Byers. We wanted Taj to experience middle school in a different environment. Taj was accepted to Greene Street Friends School.

CHAPTER 16

TAJ AT GREENE STREET FRIENDS SCHOOL

The mission at Greene Street Friends School was exactly what we wanted for Taj: to create a truly diverse community that speaks to the school's belief of the inner light residing in every child. Ron and I believed in developing the whole child. Taj made friends easily and caught on to the Quaker way, and he began expressing himself more in the classroom.

Taj developed good study habits at Greene Street, but he also had a mentor, Art Freidman, who was a champion for him. He frequently talked with Taj, encouraged him, and helped him stay motivated. Art was a guidance counselor and a great friend, and remains an influence in Taj's life today. Through it all, Taj excelled on the basketball courts at GSFS, competing against other Friends schools. Taj was most at home on the courts.

In seventh grade, he experienced the GSFS Fall Fair, a fundraiser for the kids' spring trip to Costa Rica. The Fair had all sorts of items to bid on to help with the cost of the trip. No child would be left behind; all kids would experience taking the trip to Costa Rica with their Spanish teachers. The two seventh grade classes would be away for twelve days. Some kids had never flown on an airplane. Yikes, parents were nervous. What an experience, going to school with their pen pals in Costa Rica, eating different foods, seeing different sights, experiencing a different culture. The kids were excited!

The trip to Costa Rica was a phenomenal experience. We had to be at the airport at 4:00 a.m. We'd spent weeks going over the list of supplies, making sure we had everything needed. The kids and parents slowly began to arrive at the airport, the parents nervous and teary eyed. Finally, it was time for them to board the plane. Butterflies were in my stomach. We followed the kids as far as we could, straining our necks and waving goodbye until we couldn't see them anymore. Then all the students were out of sight. What do we do now? Ron and I were exhausted so we sat at the airport for a long while in silence.

Those were the longest twelve days for us. I missed the sound of Taj's voice. We had an app to check daily, where the teachers posted an update of each day's activities. We looked forward to the daily post. The kids had an evening flight returning to Philadelphia. We arrived two hours early to the airport. We were anxious and excited to see Taj and all the kids.

It was announced that their flight had landed. Yet, it seemed like forever before we saw them since they had to go through customs. Finally, one-by-one they started to appear. There were screams of joy and exhilaration by the kids and the parents. Then we saw Taj! He had a huge smile across his face. Ron and I ran and hugged him very tight. It was a great trip, a great experience; and it was great to have him home.

Seventh grade science class always had a traditional egg drop at the end of each year. The teachers asked the students to lower an egg out of the second floor window via a long string down to a dish on the ground without breaking the egg. Gravity was to help keep the egg steady. The temperature was below freezing that morning. All the parents had to stand outside for this experiment. Our teeth were chattering and our fingers were blue as we waited for the egg to finally come out the window. It seemed to take forever! At last Taj began to slowly lower his egg; the wind sent it sideways and it cracked. Taj was disappointed, but he had lots of fun. We were happy when it was over so we could find a warm spot inside.

Eighth grade brought the immediate challenge of selecting a high school. There were applications to fill out and schools to visit. Taj had shadow days at Germantown Friends School, Friends Select School, Saint Joe's Preparatory School, and Roman Catholic High School. Ron and I also had to be interviewed. It seemed endless. Art Freidman was there for us with our many questions. What would be the right fit? What about academics? Who would have the best sports programs for basketball and baseball? We revisited St. Joe's Prep and Roman Catholic. Taj seemed to feel at home at Roman Catholic. And so we waited to hear from the schools.

One day a large envelope arrived in the mail. Taj was at school. We had to wait until he came home to open the letter. The school bus was late that afternoon due to weather. It was raining sideways. Finally Taj walked in and I said, "You have some mail on the table." Taj opened the envelope, took out the letter and began reading it. He ran, raising the letter in his hand and screaming, to his bedroom and around the condo that he'd been accepted to Roman Catholic High School. That was it! He was going to Roman Catholic. Ron and I were thrilled. A victory.

The remaining year at Greene Street was studying, playing basketball for the Hawks, preparing for their Costa Rican penpals to visit the U. S., and eighth grade graduation. We all met the pen pals on the morning they arrived at Greene Street. They stayed at different homes, and their itinerary was packed. Taj's pen pal, Sebastian, spent two nights with us. He was delightful! The exchange students went to school with our kids, attended Meeting for Worship (a weekly gathering where students sit in silence to meditate and think for thirty minutes before classes begin), and then visited many historic sights of Philadelphia. The big thrill for them was going to a 76ers basketball game at the Wells Fargo Center. They loved it! It was also exhilarating for them to have their photos taken with the Rocky

Statue and running the Rocky Steps. There was a big party before the kids had to leave, lots of testimonials of enjoyment, thank yous, and lots of tears and many hugs.

Graduation was a big deal for eighth grade that year. Greene Street had built a new addition to the building, a state-of-the-art multipurpose room. Taj's graduation would be the first to take place in this new facility. Each of the eighth graders was given a choice as to what they'd like to present for graduation. They had the option of presenting a banner, doing a performance of singing or dancing, or giving a speech. There was no way Taj would sing or dance. He told us that he'd be giving a speech for graduation. Ron and I were completely flabbergasted. Taj was relatively shy and quiet, so for him to give a speech blew us away.

Taj told Ron that he wanted to wear a navy blue tuxedo for graduation. They went shopping and found just the right tux. He was so handsome. Taj would never practice his speech with me. I would ask and he'd say, "No, I'll practice my speech at school." We had no idea what he would say or speak about.

The day of graduation we were all overjoyed, worked up, and nervous. We arrived at school and everything was abuzz. Finally, we were seated. The banners were hanging and there were performances of singers and dancers. Then it was time for the speakers. Taj was called to the podium by the headmaster. As he began to speak, Ron and I got choked up. He stood tall and stately as his words began to flow.

> "Middle school has been a journey. Even though I've been here for two years, I feel like I have been here forever. I've made great relationships with my friends and teachers. I will miss Greene Street. I would like to thank all my friends, teachers, and family for helping me get through middle school. It hasn't been an easy ride. Testing and choosing

high school was so stressful for me and my family. After we made it past the stressful moment, we finally made a decision. I chose to go to Roman Catholic High School. Two years might not have been a long time but I can still say middle school has been exciting. Just coming to school, playing sports, and hanging with my friends really has made a big impact for middle school.

This year I've had many losses but they helped a lot through the year. Some examples are my cousin Aerial who passed away from cancer. I didn't really know her, but I heard she was great at basketball and was a very smart student. My uncle Art passed away but he would always give me amazing advice and would always try to teach me how to do the Cha Cha whenever I went over to his house. Lastly, my friend and coach, John Walton who was one of the greatest mentors and coaches I'd ever had. Besides my family, teachers, and friends; these losses motivated me to do better, act better if that was in a classroom, a basketball court, or a baseball field. This year wasn't all bad either. I had an amazing time with the pen pals, a great time in D.C., and even now at graduation. This might be the end of middle school, but it is also a new beginning, a new step into high school. Whatever you do in life could be the lock or the key to the door of success. Thank you

—Taj Davis
Speech (Greene Street Friends
School, June 2019)

I was quietly sobbing with my head in my hands. Someone gave me tissues. We were so proud. The audience clapped and clapped. Taj received a standing ovation. We were overwhelmed with joy. All the Davis family came to the graduation. We received many congratulations on what a great speech Taj had given, how poised and controlled he was, and what a great kid he was.

Then he walked across the stage and received his diploma! A victory! How did we do it? How did we get Taj to this point in his life?

CHAPTER 17

TAJ IN HIGH SCHOOL AND BEYOND

The saying "time flies" describes Taj's life from the moment we arrived in Philadelphia. One day he was entering the doors of preschool, and within a flash, he was moving onto high school. The years have flown by, and he is now a part of a new journey, with new acquaintances and new friends. His high school is very disciplined and structured but welcomes its students with open arms. Unlike his middle school with its Quaker concepts, his Catholic high school operates with a different code of learning.

Ron and I have a spiritual background in the African Methodist Episcopal Church, usually called A.M.E. We attend Mother Bethel A.M.E. church of Philadelphia, founded in 1794. The church rests upon the oldest parcel of land continuously owned by African Americans. It memorializes Reverend Richard Allen, its founding pastor in a basement crypt that serves as a museum housing Allen's tomb and other intriguing artifacts. The church also has enormous stained glass windows with both religious and masonic images. Taj has served as a youth usher in their youth program (Y.P.D.) since he was ten years old. So how did he adjust to these Catholic school changes?

Taj is one of the most resilient young men that has ever existed. He has been through more in his young life than most people experience in a lifetime; what a road traveled for a seventeen-year-old. Yet, he is well-rounded, strong, and happy. Ron and I believe the answer is simple. Love. We poured all of our hearts and souls into Taj. We say a little prayer before he goes to school each morning.

Taj's high school is a three-story building with a basement. His classes are spread throughout the building, with two flights of stairs between each floor. The first period could be on the top floor, the next period could be a few floors down, or even in the basement. He has five minutes to get from one class to the other and to be in his seat present for roll call. He carries two backpacks, each feeling like it is weighted down with lead bricks inside—a baseball or basketball backpack on his chest, and a standard school backpack on his back. The gymnasium is on the top floor.

He is thriving with his studies and sports. He is one of the few kids who plays two sports, basketball and baseball. Ron and I love going to his games, cheering, clapping, and being very vocal. What a joy!

However, during his sophomore year, there was a terrible accident on the baseball field. Taj is a lefty, a pitcher, and a first baseman. At one game, Taj was on first base. The batter hit the ball to third. The third baseman caught the ball and threw it to Taj at first base. Taj jumped up and made a spectacular catch, but the batter ran with such force that he plowed into Taj at full speed and knocked him unconscious. The fear of God came over me. Ron and I were sitting outside a gated fence that we could not get into. From our seats, all we could see was Taj laying on the ground with his baseball cleats sticking straight up. I ran down the side of the fence until I could open it. Finally, when I reached him, he was out cold. The coach was talking to him, attempting to wake him up. I was hysterical but tried to remain calm. Taj was unconscious for one and a half minutes. Finally, he came around groggy and hazed. We rushed him to the nearest emergency room, where he was given a C.T. scan and told he would be all right but no school or computer screens for five days. I always have my fingers crossed and hope for a great game while praying that he does not get hurt.

The remaining school years are moving along, planning for more sports tryouts and a multitude of practices. Days are filled with school meetings, SATs, preparing for school dances (such as the Mother Son Dance), junior/senior ball, and most importantly, college counseling. However, the major event will be graduating from high school and what lies beyond.

The endurance Taj has is remarkable: hope beyond hope, a future leader of America. He has a stellar future in college and beyond. Compassionate and highly caring, Taj carries an inner light that lifts those around him. His mother has an eternal smile with her wings in heaven, knowing Taj is everything she hoped him to be and beyond. Chemaine passed the reins to Mimi and Grandbear. The reins with her light will last forever.

CHAPTER 18

A SECOND CHANCE

When a tragedy hits, everything becomes a blur. A magpie of repetitive questions flood one's mind. What happened, when, why, how? What do we do? There's a frantic pace of thoughts. Finally I attempt to settle down and sort through what has hit me like a bolt of lightning. Thinking back about my children, I wonder what went wrong? It wasn't me, or was it? I go back to the beginning of their lives and marvel through the stages: birth, first steps, first words, first day of school, play dates, ball games, elementary school, middle school, high school, and growing into a future without disruption. Now, how do we begin to process and navigate this unexpected tragedy? Two children lost, gone forever.

From this memoir you've learned that Taj is a legacy from his mother, Chemaine, that she left to us. I held him first at birth. My first and only grandson. So beautiful with a strong name, Taj, meaning crown. A crown worn by a prince. He was and is our prince.

One never recovers from a loss of a child or children. Never. Their light burns in our hearts like an eternal flame. Ron and I locked arms and said this is our journey. We had to give our all to a little guy that would be lost without us. Taj gave us a second chance. We gave Taj a second chance. Starting all over again after raising two kids wasn't easy. It took courage.

Ron and I were very fortunate. We had friends, made new friends, had family that loved us and loved Taj and helped us to stand tall.

Most of all we had faith. Our pastor, the Reverend Mark Kelly Tyler, and his wife, First Lady Leslie Tyler, were very supportive of us.

How else did we do it? It all began with Monica McGrath, my tower of strength who said, "You can do this, you will do this." Fairmount Sports Recreation Center was where we met wonderful parents with their kids, and Taj made friends. His first T-ball coach, Michelle Salerno, always gave a special party for Taj at the end of baseball season. Kate Riccardi, our good friend and photographer, always made a baseball book for Taj after baseball season; he loves his baseball books to this day. Kate takes our photos and makes our Christmas cards every Christmas. The Mal Carney's, their son Matt who Taj met on the baseball field, became good friends and that friendship continues. The Willis' and Rossers' have sons who all played baseball, and even though at different schools, they remain close friends. Nate Bryant, Billy Pierce, and Tommy Boles' families were all so supportive to us. I wish I could give names to everyone who helped us rise and conquer. Just know our hearts are deeply grateful.

My incredible husband, Ron is my knight, who first saved me from a monster guy many years ago. My best friend, the love of my life, an amazing man, who's always there in good times and not so good times. His shoulders are forever present. He makes me laugh when I need laughter and he always says to stay calm and don't quit. We say a prayer before Taj goes to school every morning.

We've spent many hours with our psychologist, Dr. Vince Gioe over the years. His guidance,words, and care continue to console us, no words can ever thank him.

What has become of this journey? How did we learn to become comfortable in the uncomfortable? The road has not been easy, picking up broken pieces from the loss of two children was completely devastating. We still feel the pain, but we also feel joy!

We took that leap of faith and jumped in with both feet. It took courage to begin parenting all over again. Despite the challenges, we're filled with hope, love, and faith. We dream, we believe, we lead, and we serve. We were given a second chance to give Taj a second chance. To right a course to better opportunities and a beautiful future. Taj is an incredible young man. In loving memory of Chemaine and Scotty, we've turned a tragedy into a victory.

EPILOGUE

LOVING A DRUG ADDICT AND SEEING THE LIGHT

Loving a drug addict is the hardest thing you'll ever do. It's devastating to watch someone you love, who fought so hard to beat addiction, throw everything away and sink back into a life that will most likely lead to jail or death. All you ever wanted was to lead them back into a clean and sober life, realizing by doing as you have before will now just be enabling them because it will show them that you will always be there to bail them out. You want to grab and shake them and yell, "What are you doing!? What are you doing?" At some point you realize that anything you could do still wouldn't make a difference. It's solely up to them! So, you sit back and watch the tragedy unfold as if you were watching a movie, feeling helpless to stop it. How did I fail this child? I promised to protect her and to protect him. You feel like you didn't do enough or haven't done enough to help, even though you know only the addict can help him or herself. Battling drug addiction is a beast for the people addicted and completely devastating for the ones who love them. It's an overwhelming loss. It's completely out of order. No parent should have to bury their child. For every loss somebody loved them. But, through the darkness there is light.

Chemaine had the spirit of an angel. She was a beautiful soul, as was her brother, Scotty. Each day I carry wonderful memories of Chemaine and Scotty. They are my amazing grace, my reason for living, the way I can continue to help others see the light in the darkness and lift those who are feeling lost.

Being a mother was my dream and I thank God for that gift. I thank God, Chemaine left Ron and me Taj. A victory. Often I dream at night and see their faces dancing in the twinkling stars. I reminisce about their growing up and wish they were still here. I wonder could I have done something different? Could I have been a better mother? They came into this world purely innocent, giving me great pleasure and endless joy. I watched them stumble and learn to walk. I watched them stand up and fall down. But all through our ups and downs we shared God's gift of love.

What have I learned walking this journey? I've learned to reach out on that long arm of faith and ask God to order my steps daily. I've learned to appreciate life along with each day. I've learned to love deeper. Being married to Ron is a blessing and a gift loving a man so willing to walk this journey with me for better or for worse. Because he is so terribly humble one would never know he is in three halls of fame: high school, college (Virginia State), and the Central Collegiate Athletic Association (CIAA). What a role model to me, his family, and the world. He is the most loving, honest, ethical, respectful, brilliant, compassionate grandbear, father, and husband that could ever exist. Ron never stops giving, never stops encouraging, and never stops saying, "Don't quit," A victory.

And in the darkness there's always light. Seeing Taj thriving and growing into a dynamic young man, playing sports and knowing he will be a future leader of his community fills my heart. His mother, Chemaine, is smiling upon him and very proud. We often talk about what a great and gifted mom she was, although she just couldn't say "No." No to the monster, no to friends that weren't friends. Such a painful loss, but from that loss comes hope. Hope that we can save someone walking that thin line of depression, an unspoken silence. Hope to let that someone know we're there for them, we care and we love them. Talk, talk, talk to your kids. Ask them about their friends, their feelings, and school. Young people don't always want to talk, but always try to keep the door open for communication.

Barack Obama said, "Yes we can." I believe we can overcome addiction. Yes, we can become stronger. Surrounding ourselves with positive people, young or old, is crucial.

So how do we move forward? How do we deal with devastating pain and loss? How do we see the light through the clouds of darkness?

There are 86,400 seconds in each day. Each of these seconds breathes a breath. There are four seasons in each year. Each season brings new beginnings, new experiences, new life. I love the changing seasons. I see bright colors in the fall, leaves floating with the soft breeze. I feel the cool, chill air of winter. I see the blooming of spring, and feel the heat of summer nights. I've not heard Chemaine's and Scotty's voices in years, but my heart has conversations with them daily. They hear my voice, and it gives me guidance. I feel their inaudible sounds. Those we love don't go away, they walk beside us everyday... unseen, unheard, but always near, still loved, still missed, and very dear.

For all those that walk this journey, you're not alone. Loving arms are reaching out to you, to us, saying yes, we can make a difference, doing the right thing when nobody's looking. Yes we can be successful. Success is about helping others, leaving a legacy, and being thankful. This is why I'm writing my memoir, to help others. To let you know I feel your pain and through that pain we can save each other. We say thank you in advance for what we know is ours. We have gratitude. The love of family is our greatest blessing. Kindness, honesty, and hard work will always prevail.

> *It's Ok, it's alright........*
> *It's Ok to be lost sometimes......*
> *You can't wait til life isn't hard anymore*
> *Until you decide to be happy.*

> —Jane "Nightbird" Marczewski

Happiness is a decision. That's why I say to you, we together embrace arms, kneel, rise, and know we have lost, but we've loved. We will never stop loving because loving is always a victory.

Success is helping others. Gratitude is thankful appreciation and kindness. We can help each other grow. We can help those less fortunate. We can help others feel stronger and be healthy. That's what this book is all about, to reach out and touch somebody's hand and help make this world a better place. Some days still feel impossible, but each day I rise with gratitude, and pray to do better and to make a difference.

Don't forget a person's greatest emotional need is to feel appreciated.
—H. Jackson Brown

Chemaine lost her feelings of being appreciated. The monster holds on so tight that it gives an emotional state of strangulation. Sometimes one cannot crawl out of the web. Her father was always there for her even though she didn't think so. Ron and I along with her brother Scotty and Matt were always there for her. When the soul is lost, sometimes it's beyond repair.

Emma Selena Davis, my mother-in-law, would travel by bus, car, train, or on foot, often in turbulent weather, to recite a poem to churches, schools, hospitals and nursing homes. On that final day as she was about to make that transition to her heavenly light her last words were "Listen to me my children and join hands, don't quit."

When things go wrong as they sometimes will
When the road you're trudging seems all uphill
When funds are low and debts are high,
And you want to smile, but you have to sigh,
When care is pressing you down a bit,
Rest if you must, but don't you quit.
Life is queer with its twist and turns

As everyone of us sometimes learns.
And many a failure turns about,
When he might have won had he stuck it out
Don't give up though the pace seems slow
You may succeed with another blow.
Success is failure turned inside out,
The silver tint of the clouds of doubt
And you never can tell how close you are,
It may be near when it seems so far:
So stick with the fight when you're hardest hit,
It's when things seem worst that you must not quit.

—Author, Unknown

After those words she closed her eyes and the victory was won. Her five children grew up, all educated with masters degrees. We will never quit. The light will shine upon us always.

That is my plight in life—to help others and to instill positive values. And, then when my final day comes, I hope to close my eyes and say I've seen the light, I've listened, I've loved, a job well done. A victory!

ABOUT THE AUTHOR

Diane Davis is a writer, consultant, and a native of Denver, Colorado, today living in Philadelphia, Pennsylvania. She is a graduate of Denver's famed East High School, which produced Oscar winner Hattie McDaniel, movie icon Pam Grier, and music legend Phillip Bailey of Earth, Wind and Fire fame. Her formal education was enhanced when she attended Colorado State University.

Diane has spent her professional life in program development and fitness motivation. She is a certified personal trainer, fitness instructor, and motivational speaker. She specializes in public speaking on enhanced health and wellness. Diane previously was Vice President and Senior Manager for several San Francisco Bay-area companies. Her leadership with these companies illustrates her outstanding diversity of knowledge and empathy to help others overcome their challenges and strengthen their physical, emotional, and mental well-being. Diane has the ability to capture and inspire the spirit of a person needing a healthy life change. Diane has also overcome major tragedy in the loss of her son and daughter in the prime of their lives. She has written *Tragic Victory* about her life experiences. Diane is married to Ron Davis, former NFL football player and the love of her life. They have a blended family of four and are raising their grandson Taj Davis who is a budding high school scholar and athlete. In Diane's spare time she enjoys exercising, reading, writing, dancing, and spending time with her family.

SUGGESTED TREATMENT PROGRAMS

I f you or someone you know are in need of help, here are a few suggestions:

- Mental Health Awareness Text: "Go" to 741741 to reach a trained crisis counselor 24/7, confidential: www.aecf.org

- Salvation Army drug and alcohol treatment: www.nowaddictiontreatment.com

- Depression Health Communities: www.healthcommunities/depression/help

- American Foundation for Suicide Prevention: www.afsp.com

- National Organization for People of Color Against Suicide (NOPCAS): http://nopcas.org/

- United Way Helpline: 1-800-233-4357

CONNECT AND SHARE

I f you enjoyed *Tragic Victory*, be sure to connect with the author, leave a review on amazon.com and barnesandnoble.com, and purchase copies for your loved ones who need encouragement.

Connect with Author Diane Davis

www.dianedavis.net

dj@djfitinc.com

CPSIA information can be obtained
at www.ICGtesting.com
Printed in the USA
LVHW080758011122
732010LV00003B/771

9 781953 535542